Rescue Dogs

Fred Zirm

A Publication of The Poetry Box®

Poems © 2024 Fred Zirm
All rights reserved.

Editing & Book Design by Shawn Aveningo Sanders
Images of Dogs provided by Fred Zirm, edited by Robert Sanders
Cover Design by Robert Sanders (RobertSandersCreative.com)

Rescue Dogs was a finalist in The Poetry Box Chapbook Prize 2023

No part of this book may be republished without permission
from the author, except in the case of brief quotations
embodied in critical essays, epigraphs, reviews and articles,
or publisher/author's marketing collateral.

ISBN: 978-1-956285-65-9
Published in the United States of America
Wholesale Distribution by Ingram Group

Published by The Poetry Box®, July 2024
Portland, Oregon, United Sates
website: ThePoetryBox.com

dedicated to:

*Woofer
Carabelle
Snuffles
Trey
Dory
and Larry*

and to rescue dogs everywhere

Contents

Dog Tired	7
Snow Sniffing	8
Obedience	9
Life Lessons	10
Bait and Switch	11
Dory the Deaf	12
Dog Dreams	13
What Dogs Do	14
Omnivore	15
Trey the Tri-Pawed	16
Communication	18
Two Dogs Walking	19
The Hunt	20
Rescue Dogs	21
A Parting Gift	23
The Call of the Wild	24
Walking the Dog	25
Conditioned Response	27
Undiscovered Country	28
First Walk without My Dog	29
Acknowledgments	31
Early Praise for *Rescue Dogs*	33
About the Author	35
About The Poetry Box	37

Dog Tired

At times the panting devotion,
the adoring gaze,
the disproportionate hurt
or happiness
become too much
to bear,
and I long for less
dependence
and more
distance.

But then again,
the cat seldom
comes when I call.

Sniffing Snow

Walking in the first real snow,
I thought my new pup's sense
of smell would be dulled
by that barrier of white,
but it was sharpened instead
as Woof buried his snout
deep into drifts to inhale
the remnants of his first fall
which winter had now hidden
and spring would uncover
along with a green
he had never seen.

OBEDIENCE

Why does my dog sit so patiently
waiting for the signal he can eat
his bowl of food but pays no
attention on a walk when I forbid
some rabbit droppings? Is *Yes*
easier to obey than *No*? Is the house
my kingdom and the world his?
Or can he only resist temptation
when it is also the reward?

LIFE LESSONS

Larry hasn't learned cats are enemies
and not all people are friends.
Larry hasn't learned he's smaller
than a Great Dane and slower
than a greyhound or that
he'll ever be older
than he feels right now.
Larry hasn't learned there's
no such thing as a free lunch
although he sometimes
has to wait for dinner.
Larry hasn't learned anything
he doesn't need to know
and knows many things
he feels no need to tell
as he skitters across the hardwood
when the doggie bowl is finally filled.

BAIT AND SWITCH

The lost *Lhasa* was so lean
and shy at the shelter
we had to take her with us

but once Carabelle put on
some pounds and made herself
at home, she became

a Buddhist bully
with her wolfman underbite
and her overbearing attitude

displacing our older dog
from his stair-side perch
baring her teeth at

one-and-done babysitters
and ignoring our commands.
It was then we realized

Carabelle was a sentinel
and our front foyer
was her Tibetan temple.

Dory the Deaf

dog sees what she cannot
hear, smells what she cannot
see, and senses the world
in ways we cannot fathom.

Dog Dreams

We often assume they are simple
and straightforward—a leg moves
and they are chasing a rabbit
a moan means a missing doggie dish.

But wonder if their dreams are more
like ours—forgetting to prepare
for an obedience exam or losing
a puppy love or finding themselves
alone on stage with the crowd
screaming for some song about a hound
dog while their father snarls from the wings.

Or, perhaps, the rabbit is chasing them.

What Dogs Do

What draws a dog
to do his business
in one spot and not
some other?

What is all that
sniffing and shifting
before the perfect
place is found?

Are they consulting
some canine Yelp
to see what's trending?

Or are they seeking
some niche that is
theirs and theirs alone?

Or, perhaps, they are
eco-hounds looking for
soil that needs enrichment?

But most often they seem
like pirates or poets, burying
supposed treasure where we must
stoop and strain to dig it out.

Omnivore

Dry dog food was enough for Snuff.
Then the vet suggested shredded
cheese with the morning meal.
Snuff's coat glowed, but
she began to nose aside
her cheese-less supper,
so we added some liver treats.
That seemed to satisfy her
until our daughter slipped her
some steak, and now Snuff disdains
her bowl completely, sitting
by the dinner table, staring at
our sirloin—and then at us.

Trey the Tri-pawed

1. Higher Mathematics

Trey does not realize
three is less than four
or, perhaps, dogs just
count things differently.

2. Momentum

The faster he goes,
the less he limps.

3. Emotion

The happier he is,
the higher he hops.

4. Priorities

Trey is always eager to please
except when there is something
good to smell there or there
or there.

5. Downward Dog

On hot summer mornings
a dive and a roll
in the dew-soaked grass
is next to nirvana.

6. Advanced Linguistics

Trey seldom barks
but yawns and yaps
canine monologues
that put Farfel to shame.

7. Friendship

Whenever I sit on sofa
or stair and Trey stands
by me, he rests his stump
on my knee. And I look into
his eyes whenever the world
seems cold.

~for Trey, d. 01/05/2024

Communication

The deaf dog barks
not knowing what
it is to hear
but longing
to be understood.

Two Dogs Walking

The younger one strains ahead
eager to see what comes next
while the older stays to sniff
whatever we have just passed,
making me the wishbone they try
to pry apart toward what they think
they want until they spot the fox
crouching in the neighbor's driveway
and wrap their leashes around me
in a momentary maypole dance,
old and young in a fine frenzy
barking now, now, now, now, now.

The Hunt

I never heard / so musical a discord, /such sweet thunder.
—Hippolyta, *A Midsummer Night's Dream*

Hounds are historians,
seeking primary sources
to sniff out who did what,
where, when, how, and why—

tracking the past,
then treeing the present
to corner their quarry
with a queer two-toned cry

like a poet near the end
of his final sonnet—
glad the mad chase is over,
sad the keen quest is done

knowing the next rhyme
could be his very last one.

Rescue Dogs

> *I tell my poetry workshop students,*
> *if you're stuck in a poem, just have a dog come in.*
> —Billy Collins

I picture a climbing party of novice poets
trapped on a narrow, wind-battered ledge.
Tied together at the waist by an overextended
metaphor, they collapse and gasp in the thin air
of abstraction, calling out for help.
At that moment, a Saint Bernard,
large pawed and panting,
scrambles over ice and rock
to offer the climbers what they need—
the chipped and weathered oaken cask
of concrete images hanging from his furry neck.

Or I imagine a lone poet, lost
in deep woods of his own devising
as he tries to follow Dante or Frost,
who have left no breadcrumbs
or broken branches.
Preoccupied, he stumbles
over a hidden meaning
and falls into an arcane abyss.
At that moment, his faithful collie
races barking to the farmhouse
where the mother, holding a dish towel, says,
"She's trying to tell us something."
"Yeah," the father scowls and strokes his chin.
"Timmy's fallen down that damn well again."
 He spits in the barnyard dust, then wipes
 his mouth with the back of his hand.
"I told him to quit messing around with allegory."

[. . .]

At this moment, my dog Snuff,
a shepherd-hound refugee
from Death Row, looks up at me
with the hurt but hopeful
eyes of the once abandoned.
I rise from my desk. Her tail thumps
the floor as I scratch her head and then
offer her the tethered freedom of the leash.
She is once again delighted
the world is just beyond our door—
and she can lead me through it.

A Parting Gift

When someone comes to the door,
Dory grabs her favorite toy
and runs to greet them
with tail-wagging hospitality.

But if they reach for that mangled
stuffed jellyfish, she darts away
after offering what she had
no intention of ever giving up.

The Call of the Wild

Woof was mostly shepherd
with just a whiff of wolf.
He would heel and stay
and lie quietly by our side
off leash while we did
some outdoor morning chores.

But if we turned our backs
too long, he'd run off to the
nearby woods to bark and bay
and roll in leaves and muck
and explore the shallow creek
until the sun was nearly set.

He always came home even
if we failed to find him first.
But these forest treks faded
when Woof's hips betrayed him.
I had to carry him outside before bed
for him to squat and sniff the evening air.

Until that time I came back
from fetching a forgotten bag,
and found Woof limping toward
the woods, whimpering softly,
and knew we had to let him go.

Walking the Dog

— *1* —

Although she's the one on the leash, I often
envy my dog's freedom when we take a walk.
She seems to see the whole world as her
territory to smell and taste and mark
everywhere. And when her inner
GPS finally finds the right spot,
she stakes a more monumental claim.

How strange I must appear to her—always
walking in straight lines on sidewalks or
on the left side of the street, facing traffic,
never stopping to sniff or squat or lift a leg,
confining my business to home—the one place
she'd never think to soil—marking the same
spot over and over, then trying to mute the smell.

— *2* —

My wife informs me I am mistaken:
our dog is not marking her territory.
Instead, she is entering into a
canine conversation—a time-delayed
meet and greet—with other dogs, past and
future, who pass this way and piss this way
before and after ours has pissed and passed.
This is not instantaneous text messaging
but a sort of liquid chain letter, a conference
call in non-real time. But the basic message
is the same as it has always been
from the caveman through Kilroy:
I was here.

[. . .]

— 3 —

If my wife is right, who started the conversation?
Was it some prehistoric proto-pup who left his mark
when this suburban street was a Neolithic hunting
trail of peers, when dog and master were newly met?

And when will the conversation end, if ever?
When some mutant mongrel staggers through
a nuclear wasteland and empties his glowing
bladder one last time before he collapses?

Or will it end when the ocean comes again
and we are all left to dog paddle our way
to some new and distant shore?

Perhaps, though, thousands of years from now
a man and his dog will walk this same path,
whatever shape it's taken by then,
and the man will think these same thoughts,
vaguely sensing they've been thought before,
making these marks we humans leave each other.

Conditioned Response

Later, whenever Pavlov heard
a bell, did he find himself
missing his hungry dogs?

Undiscovered Country

One-by-one, my dogs have run ahead
as scouts to sniff out our mortality.
They have shown me how to grow
grey and stiff and deaf—and doze all day.
As pups, they took pride in giving me
the sticks they scampered to retrieve,
while I took joy in their returning,
but once they stumbled into that deeper
sleep, they could bring nothing back to keep
me from the twitch and whimper of my own
dreams or the darkness of that final fetching.

First Walk without My Dog

I follow in her footsteps
where once she followed
mine—or rather where
we once walked together:
me, intent on exercise,
she, on exploration.

Too late, I realize
all dogs are guide dogs,
alerting us to what we
might miss, all the unseen
mysteries of place and time
in a twig or leaf or clump
of grass that tell us where
we are and who's been here before.

At the end, she refused to eat
what she could not process,
just as I cannot digest her death
and deny it still: checking
her water dish, leaving
her leash hanging by
the front door, and looking
for her to come to me
even now, as I call.

My senses are not as keen
as hers, though her absence
has sharpened them some.
I pause to sniff the breeze
she knew so much better than I
and try to read the world
as she did—alive, alive, alive.

Acknowledgments

"Dog Tired" appeared in the anthology *And the Tail Wagged On* (Lost Tower Press, October 2015).

"Undiscovered Country" won second place in the 2022 Bethesda Urban Partnership poetry contest and was posted on their website in a slightly different version.

"First Walk without My Dog" part of the collection *The Dead Pets Poetry Anthology (*Transcendent Zero Press, March 2023).

Early Praise for *Rescue Dogs*

Hark (and bark) to the heroes that pounce and doze throughout Fred Zirm's moving new collection, *Rescue Dogs*: here's Dory the Deaf, Trey the Tri-pawed, Carabelle, Larry, Snuff, Woof, and the younger one. *All dogs are guide dogs*, Zirm writes, and these fetching meditations show the deep affection and abiding insights that come from living tenderly with animals as an animal. Wry and warm, Zirm's poems remain *eager to see what comes next* while illuminating the hard lessons and gentle paradoxes of life among loss and time.

—Zach Savich, author of *Daybed*

In *Rescue Dogs,* Fred Zirm takes us on our mortal journey with dogs as both our guides and our companions. Observing the human world through their eyes—and their world through our own—his poems become the *leash* we follow to a deeper understanding of what it means to be alive. With its wit, intelligence, and profound emotion, *Rescue Dogs* deserves a place on every dog owner's—and poetry lover's—bedside table.

—Sue Ellen Thompson, author of
Sea Nettles: New & Selected Poems
and Winner of the Maryland Author Award

About the Author

After earning a B.A. and M.A. in English from Michigan State and an M.F.A. from the Playwrights Workshop at the University of Iowa, **Fred Zirm** spent nearly 40 years teaching English and drama at an independent boys' school in Maryland. Since his retirement, he has continued to direct plays at community theaters but has also focused on writing poetry and has become deeply involved with the Writers' Center at the Chautauqua Institution. His work has been published in over a dozen small literary magazines and anthologies, including *The Café Review, Still Crazy, cahoodadoodaling (*Pushcart Prize nominee), *Greek Fire, The Poeming Pigeon,* and *Objects in the Rearview Mirror.* His first poetry chapbook, *Object Lessons* (Main Street Rag), was published in January 2021.

About The Poetry Box®

The Poetry Box, a boutique publishing company in Portland, Oregon, provides a platform for both established and emerging poets to share their words with the world through beautiful printed books and chapbooks.

Feel free to visit the online bookstore (thePoetryBox.com), where you'll find more titles including:

Journey of Trees by Susan Landgraf

gOD: A Respectfully Divergent Testament by Penelope Scambly Schott

Reading Wind by Carol Barrett

When All Else Fails by Lana Hechtman Ayers

Elemental Things by Michael S. Glaser

The Squannacook at Dawn by Richard Jordan

A Nest in the Heart by Vivienne Popperl

This Is the Lightness by Rachel Barton

Self Dissection by Amelia Diaz Ettinger

The Further Adventures of Zen Patriach Dogen by James K. Zimmerman

Kansas Reimagined by Anara Guard

Now Is What Matters by Janet Steward

Jump Straight Up by Jarold Ramsey

and more . . .

www.ingramcontent.com/pod-product-compliance
Lightning Source LLC
LaVergne TN
LVHW050030080526
838202LV00070B/6989